COLORING BOOKS
FOR TEENS
WOLVES & MORE

ART THERAPY COLORING

Preview of Coloring Pages

Preview of Coloring Pages

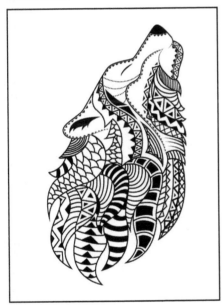
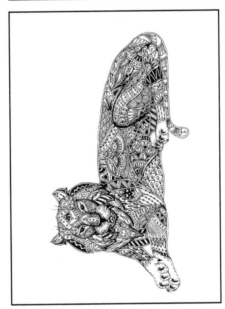

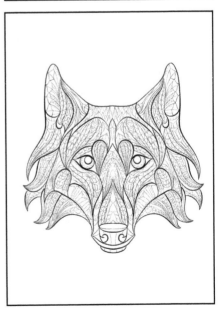

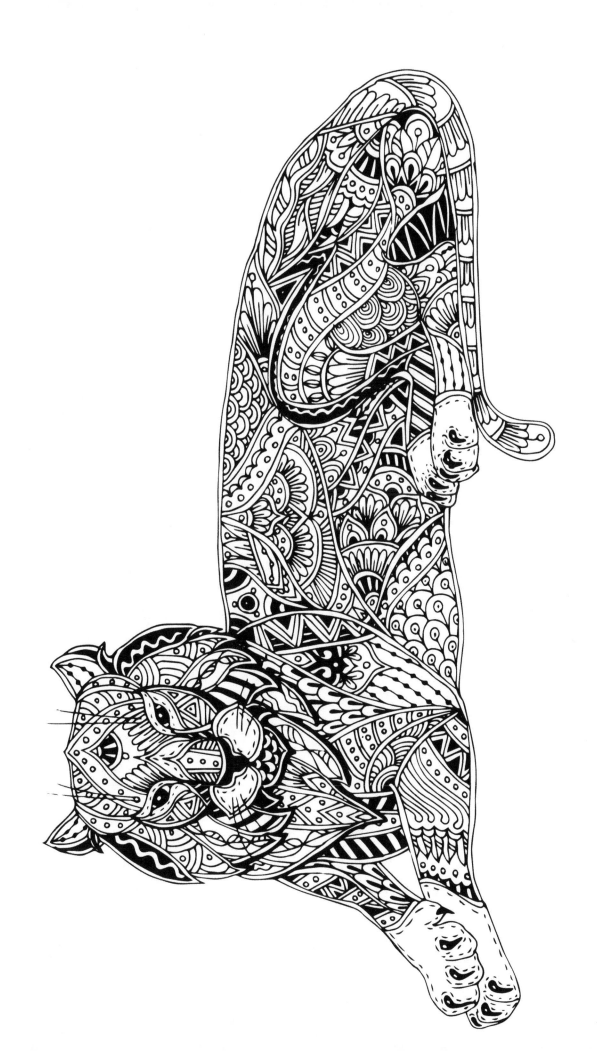

Coloring Books For Girls

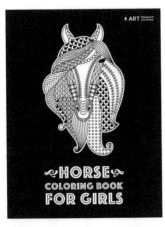

HORSE COLORING BOOK FOR GIRLS

UNICORN COLORING BOOK FOR GIRLS

COLORING BOOKS FOR GIRLS UNICORNS

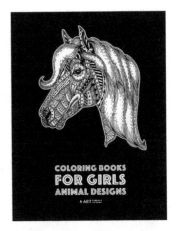

COLORING BOOKS FOR GIRLS ANIMAL DESIGNS

COLORING BOOKS FOR TEEN GIRLS VOL 1 DETAILED DESIGNS

TEEN COLORING BOOKS FOR GIRLS VOL 1

TEEN COLORING BOOKS FOR GIRLS VOL 2

TEEN COLORING BOOKS FOR GIRLS VOL 3

COLORING BOOKS FOR GIRLS CUTE ANIMALS

GIRLS COLORING BOOKS CUTE ANIMALS

COLORING BOOKS FOR GIRLS ANIMALS

COLORING BOOKS FOR GIRLS Princess & Unicorn Designs

GIRLS COLORING BOOKS DETAILED DESIGNS VOL 1

COLORING BOOKS FOR GIRLS DETAILED DESIGNS VOL 2

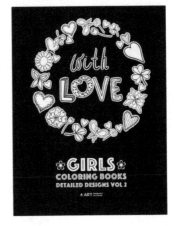

with LOVE GIRLS COLORING BOOKS DETAILED DESIGNS VOL 2

COLORING BOOKS FOR GIRLS RELAXATION Hearts

Art Therapy Coloring Books

COLORING BOOKS FOR TEEN GIRLS DETAILED DESIGNS
Black Background

TEEN GIRLS COLORING BOOKS DETAILED DESIGNS
Native American Inspired

COLORING BOOKS FOR TEENS RELAXATION
Nature Designs

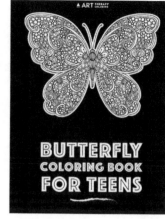

BUTTERFLY COLORING BOOK FOR TEENS

COLORING BOOKS FOR TEEN GIRLS VOL 2 DETAILED DESIGNS

ADULT COLORING BOOKS FOR GIRLS
Detailed Designs

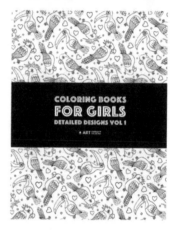

COLORING BOOKS FOR GIRLS DETAILED DESIGNS VOL 1

COLORING BOOKS FOR GIRLS OCEAN DESIGNS

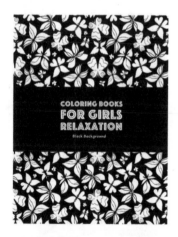

COLORING BOOKS FOR GIRLS RELAXATION
Black Background

COLORING BOOKS FOR OLDER KIDS GEOMETRIC DESIGNS

HEART COLORING BOOK FOR KIDS

DETAILED COLORING BOOKS FOR KIDS
Ocean Designs

ANIMAL COLORING BOOK FOR OLDER KIDS

COLORING BOOKS FOR OLDER KIDS ANIMAL DESIGNS

COLORING BOOKS FOR GIRLS RELAXATION
Butterflies

BUTTERFLY COLORING BOOK FOR KIDS
Detailed Designs

Coloring Books For Kids

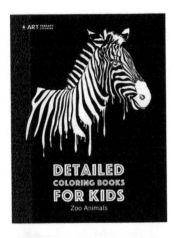

DETAILED
COLORING BOOKS
FOR KIDS
Zoo Animals

COLORING BOOKS
FOR KIDS AGES 8-12
~ANIMALS~
Black Background

DETAILED
COLORING BOOKS
FOR KIDS

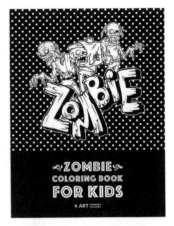

~ZOMBIE~
COLORING BOOK
FOR KIDS

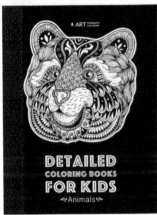

DETAILED
COLORING BOOKS
FOR KIDS
~Animals~

DETAILED
COLORING BOOKS
FOR KIDS
~Elephants~

COLORING BOOKS
FOR KIDS
OCEAN DESIGNS

MANDALA
COLORING BOOK
FOR KIDS
Black Background

DETAILED
COLORING BOOKS
FOR KIDS
~Butterflies~

~UNICORN~
COLORING BOOK
FOR KIDS AGES 4-8
Volume 1

~UNICORN~
COLORING BOOK
FOR KIDS AGES 4-8
Volume 2

COLORING
BOOKS FOR KIDS
CUTE ANIMALS

~KIDS~
MANDALA
COLORING BOOK

MANDALA
COLORING BOOK
~FOR KIDS~

~SHARK~
COLORING BOOK

DINOSAUR
COLORING BOOK

Coloring Books For Boys

COLORING BOOKS
FOR BOYS
WILD ANIMALS

COLORING BOOKS
FOR BOYS
~DRAGONS~

COLORING BOOKS
FOR BOYS
ANIMAL DESIGNS

COLORING BOOKS
FOR BOYS
OCEAN DESIGNS
Black Background

COLORING BOOKS
FOR BOYS
~SHARKS~

DINOSAUR
COLORING BOOKS
FOR BOYS
Detailed Designs

COLORING BOOKS
FOR BOYS
NATIVE AMERICAN INSPIRED

COLORING
BOOKS FOR BOYS
ANIMALS

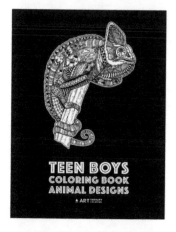

TEEN BOYS
COLORING BOOK
ANIMAL DESIGNS

TEEN COLORING BOOKS
~ FOR BOYS ~
DETAILED DESIGNS

TEEN COLORING BOOKS
~ FOR BOYS ~
DETAILED DESIGNS
Black Background

COLORING BOOKS
FOR TEEN BOYS
DETAILED DESIGNS

COLORING BOOKS
FOR TEEN BOYS
DETAILED DESIGNS
Black Background

ADULT
COLORING BOOKS
FOR KIDS
Geometric Designs

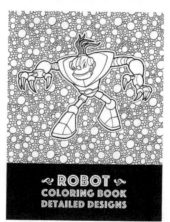

~ ROBOT ~
COLORING BOOK
DETAILED DESIGNS

DETAILED
COLORING BOOKS
FOR KIDS
Geometric Designs

Coloring Books For Teens

COLORING BOOKS FOR TEENS WOLVES & MORE

TEEN COLORING BOOKS ANIMAL DESIGNS

TEEN COLORING BOOKS ANIMALS
Black Background

COLORING BOOKS FOR TEENS OWLS

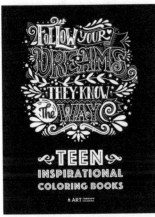

TEEN INSPIRATIONAL COLORING BOOKS

TEEN COLORING BOOKS ANIMAL DESIGNS
Black Background

DETAILED COLORING BOOK FOR TEENAGERS
Animal Designs

TEEN COLORING BOOK INSPIRATIONAL QUOTES

TWEEN COLORING BOOKS FOR GIRLS CUTE ANIMALS

ADULT COLORING BOOKS FOR TEENS
Animal Designs

COLORING BOOKS FOR TEENS CAT & DOG DESIGNS

MANDALA COLORING BOOK FOR TEENS
Black Background

COLORING BOOKS FOR TEENS SEAHORSES & MORE

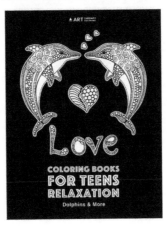

COLORING BOOKS FOR TEENS RELAXATION
Dolphins & More

TEENS COLORING BOOK OCEAN THEME

COLORING BOOKS FOR TEENS SHARKS & MORE

Coloring Books For Teens

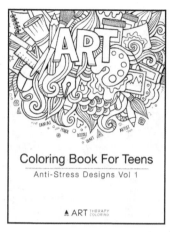

Coloring Book For Teens
Anti-Stress Designs Vol 1

▲ ART THERAPY COLORING

Coloring Book For Teens
Anti-Stress Designs Vol 2

▲ ART THERAPY COLORING

Coloring Book For Teens
Anti-Stress Designs Vol 3

▲ ART THERAPY COLORING

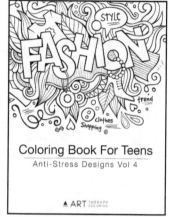

Coloring Book For Teens
Anti-Stress Designs Vol 4

▲ ART THERAPY COLORING

Coloring Book For Teens
Anti-Stress Designs Vol 5

▲ ART THERAPY COLORING

Coloring Book For Teens
Anti-Stress Designs Vol 6

▲ ART THERAPY COLORING

Coloring Book For Teens
Anti-Stress Designs Vol 7

▲ ART THERAPY COLORING

Coloring Book For Teens
Anti-Stress Designs Vol 8

▲ ART THERAPY COLORING

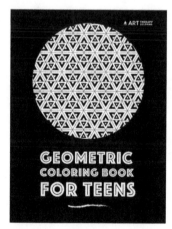

GEOMETRIC COLORING BOOK FOR TEENS

ANIMAL COLORING BOOK FOR TEENS VOL 1

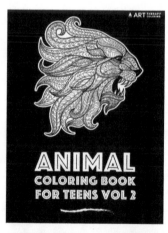

ANIMAL COLORING BOOK FOR TEENS VOL 2

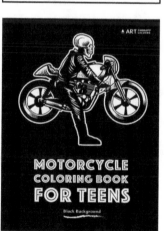

MOTORCYCLE COLORING BOOK FOR TEENS
Black Background

COLORING BOOKS FOR TEENS OCEAN DESIGNS
▲ ART THERAPY COLORING

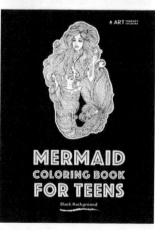

MERMAID COLORING BOOK FOR TEENS
Black Background

SKULL COLORING BOOK FOR TEENS
Black Background

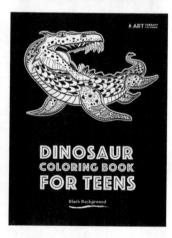

DINOSAUR COLORING BOOK FOR TEENS
Black Background

Coloring Books For Adults

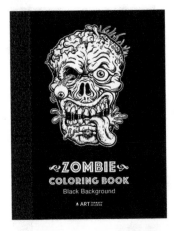

ZOMBIE
COLORING BOOK
Black Background

ZOMBIES
COLORING BOOK
SCARY DESIGNS
Black Background

DRAGON
COLORING BOOK

DRAGON
COLORING BOOK
Black Background

AFRICA
COLORING BOOK
FOR ADULTS

LION
COLORING BOOK
FOR ADULTS

TIGER
COLORING BOOK
FOR ADULTS

WILD ANIMALS
COLORING BOOK
ZENDOODLE DESIGNS

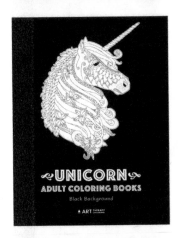

UNICORN
ADULT COLORING BOOKS
Black Background

HORSE
COLORING BOOK
DETAILED DESIGNS

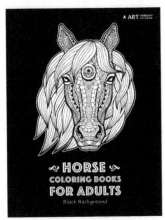

HORSE
COLORING BOOKS
FOR ADULTS
Black Background

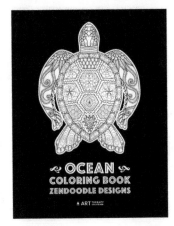

OCEAN
COLORING BOOK
ZENDOODLE DESIGNS

WOLF
COLORING BOOK
FOR ADULTS

DOG
COLORING BOOK
DOODLE DESIGNS

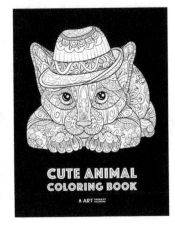

CUTE ANIMAL
COLORING BOOK

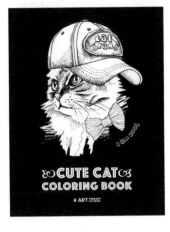

CUTE CAT
COLORING BOOK

Coloring Books For Adults

TATTOO COLORING BOOK **FOR ADULTS** Black Background

TATTOO COLORING BOOK **FOR ADULTS**

TATTOO COLORING BOOK FOR ADULTS RELAXATION

BUTTERFLY COLORING BOOK **FOR ADULTS** Black Background

NATIVE AMERICAN COLORING BOOK **FOR ADULTS**

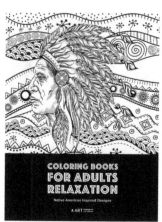

COLORING BOOKS **FOR ADULTS RELAXATION** Native American Inspired Designs

SKULL COLORING BOOK **FOR ADULTS**

SWIRLS COLORING BOOK **FOR ADULTS** Black Background

DOG & COFFEE COLORING BOOK **FOR ADULTS**

CAT & COFFEE COLORING BOOK **FOR ADULTS**

INTRICATE COLORING BOOK FOR ADULTS VOL 2

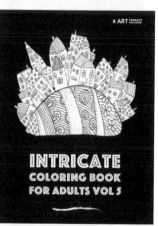

INTRICATE COLORING BOOK FOR ADULTS VOL 5

OCEAN COLORING BOOK **FOR ADULTS**

OCEAN COLORING BOOK RELAXING DESIGNS

PATTERNS COLORING BOOK **FOR ADULTS** Black Background

FISHING COLORING BOOK **FOR ADULTS** Black Background

Coloring Books For Adults

TATTOO COLORING BOOK FOR WOMEN

COLORING BOOKS FOR ADULTS RELAXATION
Hearts

ANIMAL COLORING BOOK FOR ADULTS VOL 5

ANIMAL COLORING BOOK FOR ADULTS
Black Background

OWL COLORING BOOK FOR ADULTS

COLORING BOOKS FOR ADULTS RELAXATION
Native American Inspired

FAIRIES COLORING BOOK FOR ADULTS

FLOWER COLORING BOOK FOR ADULTS
Black Background

COLORING BOOKS FOR ADULTS RELAXATION
Stress Relieving Designs

Stay Wild!
COLORING BOOK FOR ADULTS
NATIVE AMERICAN INSPIRED

Anti-Stress Coloring Book
Native American Inspired Designs

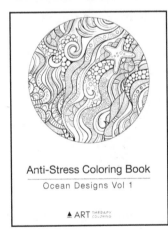

Anti-Stress Coloring Book
Ocean Designs Vol 1

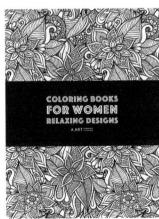

COLORING BOOKS FOR WOMEN RELAXING DESIGNS

COLORING BOOKS FOR GROWN-UPS RELAXING DESIGNS

SWIRLS COLORING BOOK RELAXING DESIGNS

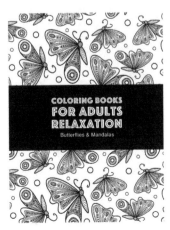

COLORING BOOKS FOR ADULTS RELAXATION
Butterflies & Mandalas

Coloring Books For Seniors

Coloring Book For Seniors
Anti-Stress Designs Vol 1
▲ ART THERAPY COLORING

Coloring Book For Seniors
Nature Designs Vol 1
▲ ART THERAPY COLORING

BUTTERFLY COLORING BOOK FOR SENIORS
Black Background

COLORING BOOKS FOR SENIORS ANIMAL DESIGNS

MANDALA COLORING BOOK FOR SENIORS

MANDALA COLORING BOOK FOR SENIORS
Black Background

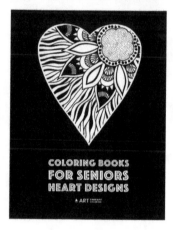

COLORING BOOKS FOR SENIORS HEART DESIGNS
▲ ART THERAPY COLORING

HAPPY BIRTHDAY TO YOU ON YOUR 70ᵀᴴ BIRTHDAY
Black Background

COLORING BOOKS FOR SENIORS SWIRL DESIGNS
Black Background

COLORING BOOKS FOR SENIORS RELAXING DESIGNS
▲ ART THERAPY COLORING

Coloring Book For Seniors
Anti-Stress Designs Vol 2
▲ ART THERAPY COLORING

Coloring Book For Seniors
Anti-Stress Designs Vol 3
▲ ART THERAPY COLORING

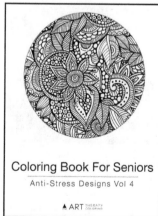

Coloring Book For Seniors
Anti-Stress Designs Vol 4
▲ ART THERAPY COLORING

Coloring Book For Seniors
Floral Designs Vol 1
▲ ART THERAPY COLORING

Coloring Book For Seniors
Floral Designs Vol 2
▲ ART THERAPY COLORING

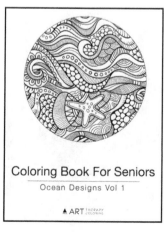

Coloring Book For Seniors
Ocean Designs Vol 1
▲ ART THERAPY COLORING

Coloring Books For Men

Coloring Book For Men
Anti-Stress Designs Vol 1

▲ ART THERAPY COLORING

COLORING BOOK
FOR MEN
ANIMAL DESIGNS

▲ ART THERAPY COLORING

COLORING BOOKS
FOR MEN
HUNTING

▲ ART THERAPY COLORING

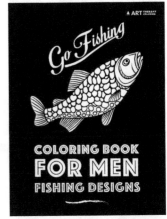

COLORING BOOK
FOR MEN
FISHING DESIGNS

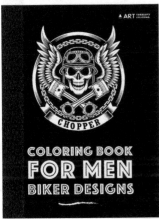

COLORING BOOK
FOR MEN
BIKER DESIGNS

COLORING BOOK
FOR MEN
SKULL DESIGNS

Black Background

COLORING BOOK
FOR MEN
TATTOO DESIGNS

Black Background

ADULT
COLORING BOOK FOR MEN
ANIMAL DESIGNS

Black Background

▲ ART THERAPY COLORING

ANIMAL
COLORING BOOK
FOR SENIORS MEN

NATURE
COLORING BOOK
FOR SENIORS MEN

OCEAN
COLORING BOOK
FOR SENIORS MEN

COLORING BOOK
FOR MEN
HAPPY BIRTHDAY

Black Background

Coloring Books For Special Occasions

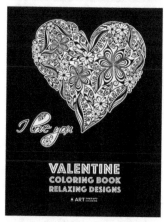

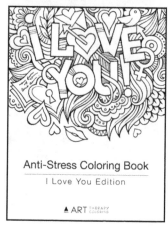

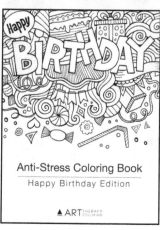

Coloring Books For Teens
Wolves & More

Published by:
Art Therapy Coloring
El Dorado Hills, California
www.arttherapycoloring.com

Shutterstock Images

ISBN: 978-1-64126-092-3